Macramé fo

Macramé Projects For Home And Garden

Caroline Piedra

Introduction

You Are About To Discover Exactly How To Get Started In The Craft World Of Macrame Like A Pro By Creating Awesome Macramé Masterpieces For Your Home And Garden!

Macrame is an effective way to bring out your creative and artistic side. It is a unique way that is used to create textiles using knots instead of knitting or weaving them. This form of art has been in existence for ages and has continued to prevail as an unrivaled form of creating simple yet sophisticated masterpieces.

Now that you are seeking to perfect or start this craft, you are probably wondering ...

What is macrame and how is made?

What do I need to get started?

Is it hard to learn macrame?

What can I make when getting started with macrame?

Do not let any of these questions come between you and creating beautiful craft items that will transform your indoors and outdoors in an instant. This book addresses all issues you might have about macrame in a very straight forward manner and using beginner-friendly language to ensure you have an easy time following what you learn!

Table of Contents

Introduction _____ 2

Chapter 1: What is Macramé? _____ 7

    History of Macramé _____ 7

Chapter 2: The Basics _____ 10

    Basic Tools and Equipment _____ 10

    Getting Started with Macramé _____ 11

    Common Terms Used in Macramé _____ 12

    Macramé Tips for Beginners _____ 14

Chapter 3: Basic Macramé knots _____ 16

    Lark's Head Knot _____ 16

    Reverse Lark Head Knot _____ 18

    Half Knot _____ 20

    Square Knots _____ 22

    The Wrap Knot _____ 24

Diagonal Half-Hitch 25

Chapter 4: Macramé Patterns 27

DIY Macramé Garden Chair 27

Macramé Plant Hanger 32

DIY Hanging Macramé Pattern 36

DIY Macramé Room Divider 40

DIY Macramé Hummingbird Feeder 45

DIY Macramé Wall Hanging 49

DIY Silk Floral Macramé Backdrop 53

Hanging Macramé Fish Bowl 57

DIY Neon Macramé Jars 60

Macramé Doily 64

Macramé Fringe Trim Pillow 69

Macramé Laptop Mat 72

Giant Macramé Rope Lights 76

Macramé Shower Curtain _____ 79

DIY Brass Macramé Hoops _____ 81

Boho Macramé Wall Hanging_____ 83

DIY Macramé Chandelier _____ 88

Macrame Inspired Clay Pots _____ 91

Conclusion_____ **94**

Chapter 1: What is Macramé?

Macramé is a technique of creating a textile using several knots to form the basic shape of the piece. You can create each knot using your hands and nothing but a mounting ring to keep your piece in place as you work.

For a project to be considered macramé, it must incorporate at least one knot that is considered macramé. In some cases, you can have the macramé element being joined using other techniques such as knitting or weaving, but in most cases, different macramé projects are pieced together using several knots.

So where exactly did macramé originate from:

History of Macramé

Macramé originates from a 13th century weavers word migramah, which means "fringe". This refers to the decorative fringes on horses and camels, which help (amongst other things) to keep flies away from the animal in the hot desert areas of Northern Africa.

Others however believe it to have originated from Turkish Makrama meaning "towel" or "napkin." It was also believed to be a way of securing the ends of weaving pieces by using the excess yarn and thread along the bottom and top edges of loomed fabrics.

One among the first uses of knots that employ macramé-style for decorating to be recorded came forth in carvings made by the Assyrians and Babylonians. The outfits of that time were caught in their stone statuary and were decorated with Fringe-like braiding & plaiting. The moors spread macramé from North Africa to Spain, which resulted in the craft spreading to France first and then throughout Europe.

In the late 17th century, it was introduced in England through the court of Mary II. Queen Mary herself taught the art of macramé to her ladies-in-waiting.

Macramé got very mainstream during Victorian era. In *Sylvia's Book of Macramé Lace* (published in 1882), which was a favorite at the time, the readers were shown how to create rich decorations both for colored and black costumes for seaside ramblings, garden parties, balls and home wear – fairylike decorations for under linens and household. Most Victoria homes were decorated with macramé. The craft was used to make household items such as curtains, bedspreads and tablecloths.

While at sea, mariners made macramé objects in off hours then bartered or sold them once they moored thereby spreading the craft to places such as The New World and China. Nineteenth-century American and British sailors used macramé to make belts, Hammocks and bell fringes. The art was known as "square knotting" named after their most frequently used knot. The sailors also referred to macramé as "McNamara's lace."

The craze for macramé had faded for some time but made a comeback during the 1970s where it was used as a means for making bedspreads, plant hangers, draperies, tablecloths, little jean shorts, wall hangings and many other furnishings. Starting in the early 1970s, jewelry made using macramé became conventional among the old and young American crowd. Using mainly granny knots and square knots, this type of jewelry mostly features natural elements like shell & bone and handmade glass beads. Bracelets, anklets and necklaces have all become popular macramé jewelry.

Chapter 2: The Basics

Basic Tools and Equipment

Let us first start with learning the tools you need to get started with macramé:

- Crochet hook and Embroidery needle – used for projects that require some fine detailing to complete a macramé pattern. The instructions for this sort of finishing are included in each individual macramé project

- Cording

- Mounting cords

- Beads – they are however optional depending on the type of project

- A measuring tape

- Scissors

- Pins such as T-pins (also called "wig" pins) – You can get T-pins at a sewing and notions store. You may also want to purchase U pins which are good for holding the heavy cords to the macramé board

- Project board or macramé board – it is the working surface you use to hold your work securely. You can get one from a craft store

- Rings to hold the mounting cords in place

*For the U-pins, you can purchase them at stores that have supplies for upholstery projects

Getting Started with Macramé

What should you do as you get started with macramé?

Determine the type of cord you need depending on your project. There are varied cords that you can use when it comes to macramé. You can use leather, twine, yarn, cotton rope or any other material that comes in an easily pliable strand.

If you are making a wall hanging, cotton rope works well. As for making jewelry, leather is great and you can use yarn to make a blanket or a scarf.

Gather a few sewing pins. You may need pins to hold the knotting material out of the way depending on the knots you will be using and sewing pins are a great option. You can also thumbtacks.

Make a project board. This doesn't need to be fancy, just something that is soft enough to push pins through and is portable. You can glue an old foam sleeping pad or a garden kneeling pad to a clipboard. You can also use Styrofoam or balsa wood.

Choose an anchor. The anchor is the piece of plastic, wood or metal that you attach the knotting material to. The anchor is usually set at the top of the project board then you use it to build on your project.

A key-ring is probably the best for making small projects such as a keychain or jewelry. A rod or a dowel will work well for larger projects

Common Terms Used in Macramé

Filler cord/ knot-bearing cord: the cord or sets of cords that you wrap the knots around

Working cord/ knotting cord: the cord or sets of cord used in making the actual knots

*Keep in mind that the working cord and the filler cord can change from one step to another in a macramé pattern.

Sennit: a knot or sets of knots worked in repeat. For instance, you have a sennit of 6 half knots if you work 6 half knot stitches in a row

Alternating: using one cord to tie a knot then switching to another cord to tie the same knot

Alternating square knots (ASK): we use this abbreviation in macramé patterns often because of the common use of square knots

Exchanging cords: this is when you change the position of the filler and knotting cords to ensure that the last filler cord becomes the knotting cords and the last knotting cords are the filler cords

Bar: a series of knots that create a raised area in your pattern design. Half hitch knots are frequently used in creating bars and they can run diagonally, vertically or horizontally across a piece of macramé work

Picot: these are the loops formed when you extend the working cords to a distance that is beyond the knot then you push them up near the knot above

Wrapping cord: this is the cord that is used to gather then wrap a group of cords. You will mostly see it at the top of a plant hanger.

Holding cord: the ring, dowel or cord onto which you anchor your project as you work on it

Fusing: the processes of joining 2 cords. It's carried out using polypropylene cord. To melt the fibers together, hold the flame from a butane lighter near close to cords then roll the tips between 2 fingers. To prevent burning, ensure that your fingers are wet first

Row: it's a line of knots that are side by side where each is tied with a different working cord

Let us look at some essential tips that will make adopting macramé easier:

Macramé Tips for Beginners

Start small: For your first project, you should begin with an easy pattern that uses square knots only. Wall hangings that are V-shaped and macramé bunting are both easy to make and look good.

Select the correct material*:* As a beginner, rope is the most suitable material for you to begin with. It is not as flexible as cotton yarn or wool and is optimal for mastering tension, attempting new knots and spacing.

Keep going: Macramé is all about getting every knot to look the same and perfecting your techniques. Tension and spacing are very crucial especially if you are going to use the same knot in forming a pattern since you can see any unevenness easily. Practice does make perfect

Find your tribe: For motivation and improving your technique, get involved in your local macramé making community and search for local craft shops which hold meet ups. You can also use social media as a platform to share tips, meet other macramé fans and learn new techniques.

Chapter 3: Basic Macramé knots

Lark's Head Knot

This knot is occasionally called cow hitch knot, and is the first knot that you need to learn. It is what attaches your macramé cords to objects like an anchor cord, branch or dowel.

How to make a lark's head knot

Bend the cord at equal lengths then position your loop against the dowel rod. Take the loop and bring it across the back then tighten by pulling the 2 ends of your cords through the loop

Reverse Lark Head Knot

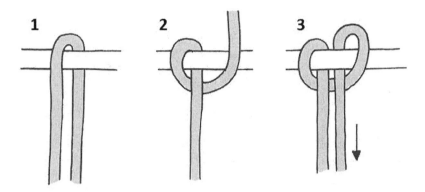

Making this note is easy, as you just have to do a larks head knot the opposite way – or you can just flip your larks head knot project around to the back.

How to make a reverse lark head knot

Bend the cord at equal lengths. Ensure that the bend is precisely half, as you will be you are going to use the rest of this cord to make the other knots. The finished project may be affected if it is not even.

Put the loop below the anchor. Bring the loop that is formed when you bend your cord in the middle below the rod or dowel with the two tips your cord on top. If working with a ring, position the loop below one side of your ring, for the loop to be centered.

Pull up the loop then pull down the cords through it. Yank the loop on top of the dowel, edge of your ring or rod then insert your finger by the loop to hold either halves of your cord. Yank the halves down via the loop so that the cords and the loop to create the shape of a pretzel shape

Make several cords for novel designs. Many projects in macramé projects will need a minimum of two sets of knotting cords. To start any new project, you will thus have to tie not less than two reverse head knot on the same anchor using two macramé cord pieces.

Half Knot

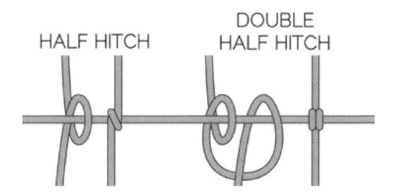

A half knot can simply be defined as a halfway square knot. Based on which side you choose to begin it on, it may be left facing or right facing.

How to make a half knot

Make the reverse lark's head knot next to the anchor. Tie the knot close to the center of your anchor – the ring, rod or dowel you are using to begin your project

Differentiate between the cords that bear knots and the knotting cords. You are going to have two cords draping down once you tie the reverse head knot. The knotting cord is the one that you move in order to create the knot while the cord bearing the knot will be the one which you fold below or above your knotting cord to create the knot.

Bend the knotting cord on the right side over cord bearing the knot. Begin close to the tips of the cords. Take the knotting cord on the right then fold it over the center cords bearing the knots. Finish this step by tucking it underneath the knotting cord on the left.

Fold the knotting cord on the left below your cord for bearing knots. Begin at the exact height as where you started the knotting cord on the right earlier. Passing the knotting cord on the left below the cords bearing the knots, pull it to the right then place over the knotting cord on the right. Yank both knotting cords until you pull the knot tight.

1.

Keep creating the half knots to form a spiral shape. A spiral will naturally occur in the cord the more you keep tying half knots with the cord. The thickness of your cord will determine the number of knots that it's going to take to form one swirl in the spiral. Tie the cord off when you obtain your desired number of swirls

Square Knots

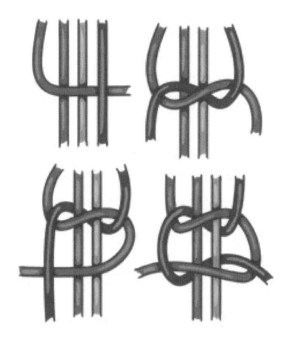

A square knot is one among the most widely used knots in macramé and it can be made as right facing and left facing.

Square knots are commonly used in macramé to form patterns. This knot needs to have at least 4 cords (2 filler cords and 2 working cords) but it can have more. The first and the final cords are called the working cords – you can call them working cord 1 and 4. The cords in the middle are filler cords and you can number those 2 and 3. These cords will change positions but will retain their original numbering.

How to make a square knot

Take the left cord then bring it over the top and to the right of the center cord thus positioning it under the last cord on the right.

Fold your right cord below the middle cord then up and out via the loop formed by the left cord.

Pull the cords tightly to make a completed half of the square knot.

Bring the right cord over the top to the left of your center cords thereby putting it under the last cord on the left.

Fold your left cord under the center cords then upwards and outside via the loop formed by the right cord.

To complete and secure the square knot, pull tightly.

The Wrap Knot

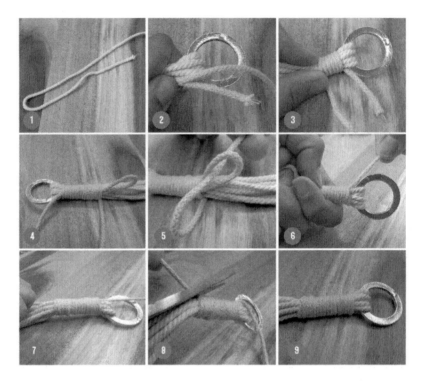

This knot is commonly used at the end or beginning of a hanging pot project and its purpose is to secure a bunch of cords together.

How to make a wrap knot

Vertically hold all the cords together.

Create a 'loop' using separate lengths of cords then lay it down at the center of the bundle of cords.

Begin wrapping the long end round and round the bunch of cords including the loop that you just made, leaving the short end to peek out the top. Ensure you wrap tightly and hold in place with your thumb.

Thread the end through the loop once you have wrapped the cords almost to the bottom of the loop.

To tuck the bottom end into the wrap, pull upwards on the end peeking out the top then complete by trimming the ends

Diagonal Half-Hitch

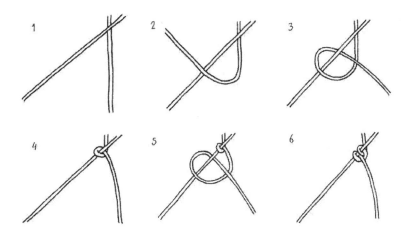

This type of knot results in a tight flat weave that is good for making enormous pieces that are tightly woven and straps.

How to make a diagonal half hitch

To make a weave slanting downwards towards the left, start making the knots from the right with the 2nd cord from your right. To tighten, loop the cord across the first cord. Loop the 3rd cord from your right across the second cord. Keep working with that exact order until your final cord then you may now start to work on the next row.

If you want your weave to slant toward the right, just have the order in reverse and start making the knots from the left side instead.

You are free to have some fun with the patterns and you may mix them in directions that are alternative into a single strap.

We will now learn some macramé patterns you can make:

Chapter 4: Macramé Patterns

DIY Macramé Garden Chair

Supplies required

Two Q plastic crochet hooks (15.75/16mm US size)

185 m (50yds) of 6mm macramé cord. This pattern used 23m (25yds) yellow, 23m (25yds) pink, 46m (50yds) green and 91m (100yds) grey

Aluminum folding chair frame

Instructions

Step 1: Start by tying the cord in a square knot near the left-hand side from the bar at the front while the chair is facing the front left side.

Step 2: draw your cord toward the back of your aluminum chair then up until you reach the bar at the top. Form a loop then draw it above the top of the bar at the top then to the back on the left hand side.

Step 4: Bring your cord to the back behind the brace and make a loop. Pull the loop above the top of the bar at the front then to the back on the left hand side as you had done earlier in step 2.

Step 5: Insert the hook in your loop then tug the loose cord until taut to make tension. Rest your hook on the frame of your chair again.

Step 6: Pull on the cord to the back behind the chair's brace then up to the bar at the top. Form another loop again.

Step 7: yank the loop above the top bar's front then to the back on the left of the final cord you made that was vertical

Step 8: Hook the brand new loop so that the loop left on the hook is now overlapping the 2 vertical cords that are on its right.

Step 9: tug on the loop until taut then yank it across the loop you had made earlier on in step 2 to create a complete chain stitch. Allow the hook to sit on the loop.

Step 10: Pull down the cord that is loose to the back behind the brace then make another loop. Pull the loop above the top of the bar at the front.

Step 11: Take the loop and pull it across the bar at the top then left of the final vertical cord you had made.

Step 12: use a crochet hook to hook the newly made loop.

Step 13: Pull the newly made loop through the loop you had made earlier in step 5 thus forming a complete chain stitch. Tug on the cord that is loose until taut then allow the hook to sit inside the loop.

Step 14: Repeat steps six through thirteen until you have made fifty nine vertical cords. At this stage, you'll probably have reached the corner at the top right hand side of your chair.

Step 15: separate your cord from the skein first by cutting to complete vertical cording leaving about 120 cm (4ft).

Removing the hook, yank the cord across the final loop. Bring down the cord to the back behind the brace then above the bar at the front and finally across the loop on your crocheting hook. Yank the cord across the loop and complete by making a square knot. Since you have a total of 60 cords that are vertical, it's now time to start cording the back of the chair and seat horizontally; they will be both done using the exact same technique

Step 16: In the bottom left hand side of where you will be working (back or seat), make another square knot. Using your cord, make a loop then in accordance the pattern you are pursuing, weave it through the vertical cording.

Step 17: yank the loop across the bar to the right then place it down under the horizontal cords that you have just created in the same way that you made the vertical cording earlier. Insert your crochet hook then tug on the end that is loose – which is currently on the left hand side – taut. Allow the hook to sit inside the loop

Step 18: Use the cord that is loose on the left side of the frame of your chair, create a loop. Pull the loop across the left bars' top then down below the horizontal cords you have newly made. Insert your hook inside the loop then tug the cord until taut. Allow the hook to sit inside the loop.

Step 19: Create another loop and keep weaving across the vertical cording in accordance to the pattern you are using.

Step 20: Repeat steps sixteen through eighteen, making sure to pull the loop you made in step 19 through the loop you had previously made on the crochet hook for every pass. Do this until you have reached the 55th horizontal row of your pattern. Complete the horizontal cording in the same way you completed the vertical cording. Your horizontal cords should now add up to 56.

Step 21: Trim the cord ends to 2.5cm to finish then melt the end of your cord using a flame and press it on the underside of your chair into a discrete location. Now all that's left is to identify a sunny garden corner to display your masterpiece.

Macramé Plant Hanger

Step 1: Start by cutting 8 cord pieces that are each five yards long. Collect the thread and cord together via the metal ring. Fold in the middle until you have 16 cord strands, each with equal lengths.

Step 2: fasten the strands of cord on the ring using gathering wrap.

For the gathering wrap, start with a piece of cord measuring 18" folding until around 6" to make a loop. With the loose ends of the cord facing up and your loop facing downwards, lay the loop on top of the bundle of cords. Holding your collection of cords and loop in one hand securely, wrap the tip of the cord that is long around the end of the loop that is shorter & loose and around the bundle using your other hand. Wrap all the way from the top to the bottom. Insert the tip of the cord which was being wrapped across the loop once you get the gathering wrap at your desired length.

To make the loop tight, hold the wrap in place then pull from the other end. Snip both ends of the gathering wrap using a pair of scissors

Step 3: To make your work easier, you can hang your macramé design on your door hook. Partition the sixteen cords into 4 sections with 4 strands each now that the gathering wrap is secure. Ensure that you group the strands adjacent to each other together. In order to ultimately prevent the various sections from being tangled, keep each portion separated using painter's tape.

To make this particular plant hanger, begin by making a half-knot. To create the half knot, you will need to work with 4 strands of cording; an outside right strand, 2 center strands and an outside left strand.

Bring the left outside strand across both middle strands. Layer the outside right strand onto the strand on the left. To form a knot, bring the right strand below the left one and both middle strands. To tighten, pull both ends. Keep tying half-knots ensuring that you always work from left to right. You will soon begin to notice a twisted design. Keep tying until you have about 10-12 inches of twisted half knots. Repeat with the other cording groups. You will have 4 chains of cascading twisted knots known as sinnets when you are done.

Step 4: We are now going to make the webbing that will hold your plant. Take one of the twisted sinnets that you had made in the step before this then separate the 4 strands of cording.

Tie a 4-inch chain of overhand knots working with 2 cord strands at a go. Do the same with the rest of the cording strands on every coiled sinnet. You will have 8 chains of knots that are thin when you finish

Step 5: To provide more support to your plant, you need to create a square knot to join together some of the chains of knots. This time you will be working from adjacent chains in lieu of working from the same initial chain or sinnet that was twisted so in order to form a V at the point of intersection of the single strands. You are going to work with 4 cord strands as with the half knot. Begin by making the half-knot then tie another half knot to have a complete square knot. This time however, you are going to work from right side to the left.

Pull the outside right strand across the 2 middle strands then apply the outside left strand onto the strand on the right. Loop the left outside strand to the back of the strand on the right and the 2 middle strands then tug to create a knot. All you have to do is repeat the half knot where you alternate working from right to left in one round then left to right the next time. This will result in a flat chain rather than one that is twisted. Keep up until your flat chain is 3-4 inches. Do this process over until you create the webbing for holding your plant and have knotted together all strands of cords that are adjacent.

Step 6: Repeat step 4 above working the sinnets that are flat to create 8 chain of knots that are each 4-5 inches thin.

Step 7: collect together every strand of cord then secure using gathering wrap. To create a tail, resize the cord to an even length. What is left is to add your plant then hang the planter.

DIY Hanging Macramé Pattern

Supplies required

Measuring tape

Scissors

Mason jar or small vase

Rope

6 in dowel

Instructions

Step 1: Cut out eight rope strands, which are 72 inches long. Take one piece of rope and fold it in half then place the end that is looped over and under the wooden dowel. Pull down the ends and into the loop. To create a lark head's knot, pull the ends tightly. Repeat this process until all 8 pieces are knotted to your dowel.

Step 2: Next, you will be making the first square knot. Beginning with the four outside rope strands, pick up the rope that is furthest on the left then fold as if to make a 4-shape. Yank the outside right strand then put on top of the strand to the left and behind the 2 middle strands then up via the loop formed between the 2 left strands. To make the first portion of your knot, tug the tips of the strands. Redo this however begin with the right strand of the four strands this time. Use the right piece to make a 4 shape then place the strand that's furthest to the left on top of it. Bring the strand on the left via the loop that is to the right then tighten to make a complete square knot. Do this with the rest of the strands.

Step 3: Next, we are going to make square knots that are alternate. This is done by reworking the square knot making process except that you jump the first two rope strands on the outside. Leave out a space of about ½ inch between the 1st and 2nd row of knots. On the 2nd row, you only need to make 3 square knots. You should be having five square knot rows that are alternating between every row.

Step 4: Next, we will be tackling the knots which are going to hold your vase or jar firmly. Put the mouth of the vase or jar below the base row of your square knots then measure halfway down the vase/jar. Using the four center strands, create a square knot. Make the knots a bit below the center knot on both sides. Pull the 2 outer strands next from both sides and create a square knot exactly above the center knot against the rows of knots at the back.

Step 5: Next, you will be working with the 2 right outer strands from the back row and the 2 outer strands from the recently made knot make a square knot roughly around the center of your jar. To have a better clue as to where you will be making the knot, place the jar within the opening. Repeat with the opposite side.

Step 6: Take your rope and cut out a piece that is about 28" long then fold to form a U shape in order to get a tail that is approximately 3" long. Collect the entire rope together at the base where your jar will sit then put the U shaped rope you just created on top. Wrap the end of the U shaped rope that is long all-round behind the rope you gathered multiple times till you get to the tip. Next, you need to yank the tip of the wrapped rope inside the loop that is below the rope you wrapped. Trim the tips of your rope on both sides of the rope that is wrapped once you have tightly pulled the knot. Finish by cutting the tips of the rope that's loose to make it even

DIY Macramé Room Divider

Supplies

Scissors

Three 3" hook screws

Wooden dowel measuring 1" x 36"

700 feet of ¼ inch three-strand cotton rope

Optional: air plants

Instructions

Step 1: For this particular project, you need to cut out twenty four strands each measuring 28 inches long. This will produce a wall hanging measuring approximately 7 inches from the dowel at the top to the one at the bottom. You can increase its length with a fringe at the bottom. Even if you want to create a piece that is shorter, it is always a good idea to have extra rope than what is required for the project.

Step 2: Do 2 larks head knot then make the beginning of a third one. Each knot will require 2 strands of rope for 12 knots in total. Take 2 strands of rope then fold them into 2 equal parts then put the middle of this pair on top of the first wooden dowel. Wrap the strands around the dowel then pull down on the ends that are loose through the loop.

Keep adding the rope strands in pairs to your dowel till you are done. Keep in mind that you are consistently wrapping over the dowel's top. If you are not keen and end up wrapping one below the dowel, it will alter the appearance of the pattern. Ensure equal spacing between each of the completed larks head knot.

Step 3: To add subtle contrast, a half knot is incorporated further below the design but it is also the first step in creating a square knot that is why it comes up first. This knot requires

4 rope strands. The 2 outer ropes pull away only a little while the 2 middle ropes stay where they are.

In the left outer rope, create a bend then move it towards then below the outer rope on the right side. Fold the outer right rope where the left outer rope crosses it, then behind the 2 middle ropes and finally up via the bend formed by the left outer rope. This pattern uses this particular knot by itself for a little while yet it's also half of the knot that you will be using for the first portion of your divider.

Step 4: This knot is made up of 2 half knots. Redo the similar pattern as in the step 3 however tug on the outer 2 strands of rope until you have the half knot that you just made resting against the first one snugly. And there you have it, the square knot. For the first row of knots, do this over on every pair of your strands of rope.

Step 5: In your first row, you should be having twelve square knots. To make the 2nd square knot row, you will use 2 strands from a single square knot and 2 other strands from the next square knot that is right beside it to form a fresh square knot which joins the 2 together. You can begin from one side then move your way across or you can start at the center of your project then work your way out on both sides. You will have an extra pair of rope strands on both sides when you reach the edges of your second row. You need to pay close attention to the space you leave out between every row when you are adding in your knots. Try not to tie your knots closer to each other together otherwise the resulting wall hanging is going to be lopsided. It helps sometimes to take a step back (around 6 feet) and inspect your design before moving on. It's better to detect the defect sooner when it is small rather than later when it's plenty crooked to be irritating.

Step 6: For this specific project, allow a space of about 2.5 inch between all your knots in order for your room divider to have an airy and light feel. You will be back to your initial pattern of utilizing every strand when you add in your third row of knots. The space created by the outer rope on the extreme left side of the divider then on the right hand side is supposed to be 2 times as long as that and then some. It should have sufficient slack for forming a scallop shape. The shape of the scallops should hold but if they do get heavy in some other parts but it is still okay. Just try to the best of your ability.

For this pattern, do 4 square knot rows that are alternating then switch up and do 6 half knot rows that are also alternate. Finish the remaining divider with thirteen other alternating square knot rows. You will require making more larks head knots to incorporate the dowel that goes at the bottom to the divider. Since you cannot make them in a similar way as when you began, you will be doing them backwards. This is how you do it: disjoin 4 strands below one of the square knots then set aside 2. Take the other 2 strands and wrap them on your dowel all the way until you have wrapped inside and beyond the tip of the same 2 strands. Wrap the strands on the opposite side and behind the back of your dowel. Keep wrapping around the dowel's front then tuck below the loop that was just created. This will create a fringe below the backside of your dowel. That's only one of the 2 larks knots that you will be making on each square knot. Take the other 2 strands from that same square knot and bring them back over then wrap them to the left hand side and around your dowel. Wrap the strands beyond the top behind your dowel then back around and beneath the newly formed loop. Scoot the knot you have just completed near to the one you created first and ensure that things are taut consistently. Do it over with every other strand in all the remaining square knots.

Trim the fringe to your desired length.

DIY Macramé Hummingbird Feeder

Supplies

Water and sugar

Outdoor Wire Hook

Scissors

Clear bottle

Macramé cord

Hummingbird feeder tube that has a stopper

Optional: spray paint

Make time: 1 hour plus drying time

Instructions

Step 1: Begin by tying a loop of cord that can fit around your bottle's neck snuggly. Create a square knot by tying the right hand side against the left then do the left one against the right.

Step 2: snip off the tips of your knot.

Step 3: Cut 4 cord pieces, each measuring around 3 yards then fold them in half. Place the halfway point of first cord through your loop. Yank the tips of that first cord under the loop then through itself thus securing it inside your loop. Tug until taut

Step 4: Redo the step above with the remaining 3 cords. Take the initial loop and fit over the bottle's neck. You should now be having 4 sets each of 2 cord lengths.

Step 5: bring one cord from the right of one of the sets and the cord to the left from the set on its right then tie them together that is approximately two to three inches from the square knots before them using a square knot. Redo the process above with the remaining sets.

Step 6: Redo step five using another collection of square knots. You will begin to notice a net-like pattern manifesting in your cords.

Step 7: Take 2 cords from a single set then form a loop around the left cord using the cord on the right, below then finally across itself. Yank until taut. Redo that process until you get to the tip of your right cord. You will notice a spiral pattern beginning to form. Clip your cord's tail once you reach the end.

Step 8: redo the above step with the remaining 3 cord sets.

Step 9: Tie all cords into a knot just a few inches over the tips of your spirals to leave a loop over the top from where you will be hanging the feeder.

Step 10: This step is optional. With the bottle removed, spray paint parts of your cord to make some colorful parts.

Step 11: Fill your bottle with four parts water and one part sugar after the cord is dry. Place the hummingbird feeder tube inside the bottle then place the bottle inside your macramé hanger.

Step 12: Clean up the surface where you want to position the hook.

Step 13: strip off the liner that is blue then incorporate the adhesive on your hook.

Step 14: strip off the liner that is black then press your hook for 30 seconds against that surface. Hang your hummingbird feeder after allowing it to cure for 1 hour.

DIY Macramé Wall Hanging

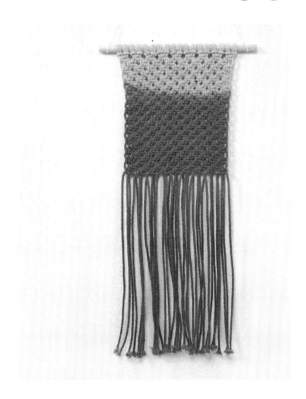

Supplies

Liquid dish soap

Salt

Plastic gloves

Metal or plastic container

Liquid fabric dye

Scissors

12 inch wooden dowel rod

3 mm cotton Macrame cord

Instructions

Step 1: Begin by cutting any number of cord lengths that is even. This pattern made 18 pieces each around ten feet long. Attach all the cords onto the dowel next using a larks head knot. Do this by folding the cord in half then place the end that is folded over behind the dowel. Finish this step by yanking your ends through the loop. This is a really conventional method of attaching the macramé cord to the starting ring or dowel. Use this method to attach each of the cords onto the dowel.

Step 2: The remaining part of the wall hanging is going to be made by only 1 type of macramé knot – square knot. Use the 2 outside strands for tying a knot around the 2 middle strands. Cross the strand on your left hand side over the 2 middle strands. Bring the strand on the right over the one on the left, below the 2 center strands then up right across the loop created by the strand on the left. Pull taut.

Redo this on the other side: crossing the strand on the right over the 2 center strands. Bring the strand at the left side over the one at the right, under the 2 center strands then up via the loop created by the strand on the right. Pull taut.

Create square knots across the entire rod for the first row. Beginning with eighteen cords; this pattern makes a total of 9 square knots for the first row.

Step 3: All the square knots are going to be made using 2 strands from 2 square knots that are adjacent for the 2nd row. For this row, the strands that were middle strands in the first row will now be the strands on the outside. When you alternate rows in such a way, you will get a nice mesh pattern in the final piece. Create a knot in between all square knots in the first row. Do not use 2 strands on either sides for this 2nd row of knots. The second row should have 8 square knots.

Step 4: For the third row, the square knots are going to be made in between the knots from the row that precedes it (total 9 knots). The strands around the edges not used from the row that came before, are again going to be used on this row.

Step 5: Keep forming the knots in this sequence until your project is to your desired length. This pattern worked 23 rows to create a complete project that is approximately nine inches long without including the fringe or dowel.

Step 6: Finally trim your fringe then even it out using a pair of scissors. You can cut the tails as evenly as you want or go for a point, steps or a more organic look.

Your project is complete at this stage if you want your piece to retain its natural cotton color.

Step 7: Dip dye (optional). For this pattern, I decided to go for an ombre dip-dyed look which is really easy to achieve. First, fill a container with hot water then add a teaspoon of dish detergent and a cup of salt for dying cotton.

Pour in the liquid dye (I used about half of the bottle) next and gently mix. (Ensure you have your gloves on to protect your hands).

Step 8: Wet the macramé first before you place it in the dye bath. Begin by first dying the bottom third or so of the piece for about 10 minutes then move a bit more down for 5 or so more minutes. Finally, quickly dip the last couple of inches in the dye briefly to have the lightest color at the top. Finish by rinsing the dyed macramé under cool running water until it runs clear.

The macramé wall hanging is ready to hang once it has dried.

DIY Silk Floral Macramé Backdrop

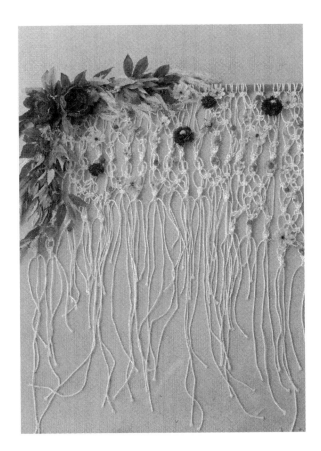

Supplies

Hot glue gun

Scissors

Silk flowers + preserved flowers

Rope (3/16 inch packets of 100 feet- 5packets)

Wooden dowel

Instructions

Step one: Cut the rope into strands that are ten foot long. (If you would like your macramé design to be longer, cut longer pieces. In this pattern the pieces cut out were 20 with a length of approximately ten foot then included a few pieces that were longer along the side later on to display the bell curve that is U-shaped. Straighten out the rope before placing it under the dowel.

Step two: draw your rope by the loop.

Step three: To attach onto the dowel, pull the rope taut then do it all over again.

Step four: While focusing on 2 loops of rope at a go, bring the rope that is on the extreme right side over the 2 strands in the middle then below the strand that is on the extreme left.

Step five: Rework step four but begin with the side on the left this time. Weave the rope on the left below the 2 center pieces then yank by the right loop.

Step six: Pull until taut and you have just made the base knot – which is commonly known as the square knot. Using pairs of 2, redo across your dowel.

Macramé for Beginners

Step seven: We will be using the exact square knot as the one above so this part is not that tricky once you have mastered that. In order to avoid getting confused, collect groups of 3 knots on your dowel to help isolate them. Separate the outer 2 strands on the right hand side and then separate the 2 strands on the furthest left as well. This will help in honing your point of focus since you will not be using them at all. Work the square knot 2 more times.

Step eight: Make only 1 square knot heading towards the center.

Step nine: The first portion of your design is typically complete. You are then going to work a row of three once more – like you did when attaching the rope on your dowel.

Step ten: proceed with the pattern. It goes this way: row of three knots, two knots, one knot, two knots, three knots and finally half hitch spiral. After that, continue with the pattern again. To make a U-shape that is more curved on the general formation, extend the pattern on the outside.

To mix your knots up a bit you can add the "half hitch spiral" knot. It's typically the same as the knot done for the other piece of your design however instead of alternating sides, you just continue to knot from the one side. It's kind of like French braiding –except without having to pick up new strands of hair from the side on the left and simply continue the braid with hair from the side on your right.

Use a hot glue gun to incorporate all your floral decorations to the backdrop for the last step.

After that you may hang the backdrop on the wall by adding extra rope to all the end points on your dowel then hang it from a hook or nail

Hanging Macramé Fish Bowl

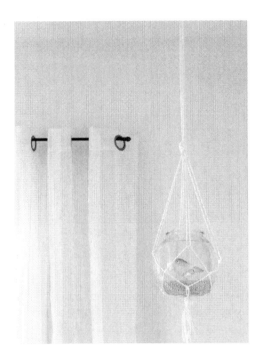

Supplies

Ceiling hook

Scissors

Plastic or glass fish bowl (this pattern used a half gallon glass bowl)

50 feet nylon cord

Instructions

Step one: Cut out 8 strands of cord measuring five feet long each. Collect each of the strands all the pieces of cord then tie a huge knot on one of the ends, ensuring that you leave out 1 to 2 inches loose over the top.

Step two: Divide your cord into 4 parts, with each section containing 2 strands of the cord.

Step three: use 2 cord pieces from one section to create a double knot and leave out a gap of 2 inches between the initial big knot that you had tied.

Step four: redo the step above using the 3 strands of rope that are remaining.

Step five: Combine one piece of cord from a section with a piece of cord from a neighboring section by tying a double knot 2 inches away from the knots you had previously tied.

Step six: For the rest of the sections, repeat step 5 using 1 cord strand from 2 distinct sections.

Step seven: Repeat steps 5 and 6. Combine 1 cord strand from a section with a piece of cord from the section right beside it using a double knot 2 inches apart from the preceding knots. For the rest of the sections, redo this process.

Step eight: Position the fish bowl over the cords that are knotted centering it on the initial big knot. Yank the ends of your cords that are loose up then around your fish bowl. Now your bowl should be resting safely in the area that is knotted.

Step nine: combine all 8 pieces by tying a knot again approximately ten to twelve inches beyond the top of your fish bowl ensuring that you leave out sufficient space for pulling the bowl out and in for cleaning. At the tips of the cords that are loose, tie another knot then yank it taut.

Step ten: Choose where you want the fishbowl to hang then put a ceiling hook. Slide the hook under the top knot between the 8 pieces of cord. To hold the hanger in place, ensure that 4 pieces of cord are on either side of the hook.

Step eleven: Place your fish in the bowl in the hanger and that's it

DIY Neon Macramé Jars

Supplies

Measuring tape

Hot glue gun

Exacto knife

Scissors

Washi tape

Aluminum foil pan

Empty jars

Neon cord

Instructions

Step one: Cut out 5 cord strands each of about 6 inches then fold in the middle. Create an overhand knot so that you are now having ten 3 cord strands. This size is abundantly sufficient for a pickle jar – adjust these lengths accordingly if the jar you are using is bigger or smaller. You may also try out using more strands for bigger jars and fewer strands for jars that are smaller.

Step two: If once you cut your cord it develops the tendency of fraying, use a lighter or tape to avoid fraying further.

Step three: Tie together 2 strands approximately two inches from the initial large knot using your measuring tape. Redo with the other strands.

Step four: Rework the above step, though you have to disunite the strands that are joined and tie together strands from adjacent knots also approximately 2 inches apart thus forming a net.

Step five: It is recommended that every once in a while you check on how your jar fits over the macramé net. If you would to alter the look of your net, just unbind the knots you are not happy with then retie using unique measurement.

Step six: Keep tying the knots as you check whether it fits the jar.

Step seven: stop tying the knots when your net gets to the mouth of your jar.

Step eight: Attach the double cord strands below the jar using the hot glue gun. To allow the jar to stand flat, this should be done in a concave area which is not going to touch the table.

Step nine: slice off the large initial knot using the exacto knife.

Step ten: The jar is going to have the ability to sit flat on a table once you cut off the large initial original knot. Use extra hot glue to secure the raw edges that have just been cut if your cord frays a lot.

Step eleven: Attach the cord to the threads at the jar's mouth using a hot glue gun

Step twelve: slice off any extra cord using the exacto knife.

Step thirteen: Use the hot glue gun to prevent any raw edges from fraying as before

Step fourteen: Measure the circumference of the mouth of your jar then cut out an aluminum strip of that is ½ inch longer than the circumference of your jar's mouth; . the threads of your jar should at least be covered by the width.

Step fifteen: If the strip of aluminum has raised bumps, use your scissor's handle to flatten them by rubbing it from the front to the back until it is smooth.

Step sixteen: When you are done, there may be some texture left but don't worry as it will in fact make the rim more aesthetic.

Step seventeen: Secure the strip of aluminum to your jar's mouth using hot glue, and you are done. You can repeat this pattern with any other jars you want.

Macramé Doily

Supplies

260 yards of rope

Size: diameter of approximately 15" plus fringe of 1-2 inches

Instructions

Step 1: Incorporate two threads to the craft pillow each three yards in length. Use a third thread that is three yards long as well to make a square knot on them. Take a different thread that is also three yards long to be the cord at the base for one row (a circle to be precise) made using double half hitches.

Take one the ends end of your working thread, create a double half hitch then using a lark's head knot, incorporate another three yard cord.

Use the next cord to create a double half hitch then add another three-yard long cord. Redo steps four to five by the end of which you will have added a total of four additional threads. Use a simple overhand knot to unite the tips of the cord at the base. Separate each of the ends on six parts (each three threads). The first thread is going to become the base cord then you use the other two cords create two double half hitch knots on it.

Step 2: On the same base cords, create two other double half hitch knots. Take another cord that is also three yards in length to become the foundation of the following row of double half hitches. Your pattern is going to be: one double half hitch that is created using a base cord + attach three additional cords 2 yards in length + two double half hitches using two working cords.

Step 3: In sections of 3 threads, divide each of the cords. With each 3 cords, create square knots (1 base cord, 1 working cord on either sides or 1-1-1). Use two working cords to create a chain braid that is short which consists of four alternating right and left loop knots. Make square knots (using the 1-1-1 design) again on each three threads then another chain braid that consists of six loop knots.

Step 4: Now make a new base cord by taking a cord that is three yards in length and create a double half hitch knot on it with all your cords plus two more cords that are one yard in length between each three double half hitches.

Ensure that the doily is lying flat on a surface and the base cord is not that tight. If necessary, you can spread the knots out on the base evenly. Your entire doily will begin to curl up warp if the base cord is too tight. Use the overhand knot to connect the ends of the base cords. Your circle should now be having 128 ends.

2 center strands are going to become base cords; direct the threads outwards then create three double half hitch knots on all 3.

In the middle of two base cords and two working cords on either side, or in simple terms 2-2-2, create a square knot

Keep going with the diamond design: direct the two base cords inward then make three double half hitch knots on either sides; the working cords will be the cords from the square knot in the middle.

Step 5: Add 2 extra cords that are one yard in length each on the foundation cords.

Use two loop knots that are alternating to connect the base cords. With each of the eight cords in your circle, repeat making the diamond pattern to have a total of 16 diamonds.

Step 6: Now create the diamond design on twelve cords – between every two diamonds from the 1st row (in simple terms, six cords from either sides).

Begin with 2 loop knots that are alternating then again make a square knot and diagonal hitches (2-6-2) in a center. Complete with two loop knots. Redo this process 16 times. Attach another cord three yard in length 3-yard long cord to become the base for the last double half hitch circle. Using all your ends, create double half hitch knots on the cord at the ensuring that in between each 2-diamond patterns, you add two cords that are two feet in length. Use a lark's head knot to incorporate them onto the foundation cord. Again, remember to keep your doily flat and don't tighten the base cord. Separate all ends in 6 cord sections, then with each section make a 1-4-1 square knot or 3 alternating loop knots.

Use the chess pattern to create the 1-4-1 square knot in the next row.

Step 7: Add another base cord for the last time then make double half stitches on it with all your cords. Create a fringe by evenly cutting off the tips to a distance of 1 to 2 inches from the final row.

Using a paint brush you can paint your macramé doily with fabric dye

Macramé Fringe Trim Pillow

Supplies

Fray Check

Fabric Glue (we used Liquid Stitch)

Washable fabric pen

Fabric scissors

Yard stick

An assortment of decorative fringe-y trim

A zipper pillow cover made from plain linen in the dimensions of the pillow insert

Instructions

Step 1: Lay out your pillow cover. Cut out your first fringe row in the same width as the pillowcase. You don't need to actually measure just line them up and begin cutting.

Step 2: Lay out the remaining rows and cut them to adjust to length. Take time to rearrange them until they are the size you want them be on the completed design.

Step 3: Make small markings on the edges where you will be applying the line of glue this way you may use a yardstick to join the dots thus forming a straight line using your fabric pen after you remove the fringe trim.

Step 4: Ensure that you follow every instruction on the fabric glue then squeeze strip of glue that is even on one of the lines you drew out with your pen. Begin on one of the ends then squeeze down on the fringe trim carefully while you continue. If it is not all flat it's still okay as you will have time to make adjustments before your glue dries out.

*Note: if you are familiar with how the sewing machine works you may it use in place of the fabric glue.

Take a step back and ensure that the lines are even and straight, adjusting where needed then glue the remaining rows in a similar way.

Step 5: Repeat these processes on the backside of the cover so that they are identical to one other. To keep the trim from fraying, use fray check on the edges.

Fabric glue dries quite fast when touched but you can give it a full day before messing with it to be on the safe side.

It is recommended that you dye the pillow cover and the fringe separately before affixing the fringe trim to the pillow.

Macramé Laptop Mat

Supplies

Wooden board

Yarn: 144m (42.5 ft) phildar phil cord (100% cotton)

Measuring tape

Scissors

4-5 clips

Size: 25cm x 45cm

Instructions

Step 1: Measure forty eight strands of yarn in length and cut out. To begin knotting, use 4-5 clips to secure the strands onto a wooden board leaving approximately 10cm of yarn.

Step 2:

Row 1: make twelve square knots from the left side to the right one.

Row 2: Leave out the first two strands. Use two strands from the square knot you tied initially and two other strands from the first row as well but of the 2nd square knot to create a new square knot. Continue knotting until you obtain a total of eleven square knots in that row.

Row 3 to 10: leaving out the first two strands for row 4, 6, 8 and 10, create rows of square knots.

Row 11: Finish one row with horizontal double half hitch.

Row 12: leave out three strands then make the following five square knots.

Row 13: Skip five strands then make the following four square knots.

Row 14: Skip seven strands then make the following three square knots.

Row 15: Skip nine strands then make the following two square knots.

Row 16: Skip eleven strands then make the following one square knot.

Go back to the row 12: make ten double half hitch diagonally down from the left hand to the right using the third strand as your holding cord. Tie ten more double half hitch diagonally down from the right hand side this time to the left using the twenty fourth strands as your holding cord. Jump the 25th strand then make the following five square knots.

Go back to the row 13: Skip strands 25 - 27 then create the next four square knots.

Go back to the row 14: Skip strands 25 - 31 then create the next four square knots.

Go back to the row 15: Skip strands 25 to the 31 then create the following two square knots.

Go back to the row 14: Skip strands 25 to the 33 then create the following single square knot.

Go back to the row 12: Create ten double half hitch diagonally down from the left side to the right using strand 25 as your holding cord. Make ten double half hitch diagonally down from the left to the right once more using strand 46 as your holding cord.

Row 13 to 21: To make the diamond pattern, create square knots.

Continue to knot using diagonal double half hitch and square knots until you get the pattern

33rd row: Finish one entire row using horizontal double half hitch.

Row 34 to 43: leaving out the first two strands for rows 34, 36, 38, 40 and 42, create square knot rows

Step 3: Cut off both ends neatly then even to your preferred length

Giant Macramé Rope Lights

Supplies

For the large rope get 35 yards which should easily cover fifteen feet of lamp cord

For the rope that is smaller, get 40 yards, which should cover 8 feet. The thickness however will obviously play a huge role in how far the rope will go.

Step 1: Begin by securing the lamp wire. To keep it stable, you should tie the wire around something such as a doorknob or the back of a chair. Place the middle of your cording behind your lamp wire. Pull the left side over the lamp wire's front then below the right hand side of the cording to create a tiny loop on the lamp wire's left side. Place your right cord at the back of your lamp wire. Yank the whole length of the cord by the tiny loop that you made on the lamp wire's left side. Repeat as much as you would like. The design will begin to spiral as you continue making more knots. The spiral will go in the same direction provided you begin from the left hand side then bring it beyond the lamp wire's top. If you put the left side under or bring the right hand side over, your spiral is going to switch directions and you will need to untie the knots. Once you are done with all your knots, what follows is wiring the socket. If you want, you may do this prior to knotting; it's entirely your choice.

Step 2: You will require some kind of planter or cup for the socket cover. For the lights, you can try using a clearance cup that is plastic and a thrifted copper cup. This is just an idea, you may use whatever you want to make your own style – ceramic planter, wooden bowl, there's really no limit.

Step 3: To begin, drill a hole underneath your cup. Incorporate the nipple that is treaded onto your socket base – to prevent your socket from unscrewing when you twist the light bulb, ensure that the tiny screw inside is tightened.

Place the washer, followed by the cup then lastly the base of your socket onto the lamp wire.

Incorporate the socket in accordance to the manufacturer's directions and then screw your washer to the nipple that is threaded.

Step 4: Slide up your rope (if you wired your socket before you began making the knots, this is the only adjustment that you will not have to do) and around the threaded nipple's end. Glue it in place.

Macramé Shower Curtain

Supplies

Macramé lace

Shower curtain – white in color

Fabric scissors

Sewing machine or Fabric glue

Fray check

Instructions

Step 1: Find a macramé lace strip and cut it to be the same length as the base of your curtain. Pin the macramé lace wherever you prefer along the base of your curtain. To ensure that your lace's top is even with the base of your curtain, use a ruler as you go.

Step 2: Working with a ruler once more, attach and pin the following line of lace. Redo with every layer that you want to integrate on the curtain. To secure, apply fabric glue along the edge at the top of every piece or you can use a sewing machine for sewing along the line at the top.

To prevent the tips of all macramé pieces that are cut from unraveling, add some fray check then hang up the curtain.

DIY Brass Macramé Hoops

Supplies

Brass Wire

Macramé Hoops in assorted Sizes (the more hoops you have the bigger your piece of art)

Pliers

Instructions

Step 1: to start, lay out the rings in your desired pattern on the floor. You should use distinct sizes in order to fit them up together similar to the way a puzzle works. For this part, just about anything goes. Create a pattern you desire and is in your preferred size.

Step 2: when all the pieces have been laid out, use your brass wire to connect the hoops together. For each attachment point, you are going to require approximately five inches of wire. Tightly wrap your wire around the 2 hoops where they intersect using your pliers.

Keep wrapping your wire around the points of attachment on every hoop until all hoops are connected to one another in one huge piece.

Your piece of art is now ready to be hanged.

You may use monkey hooks or thumb tacks for hanging your macramé art on the wall. The piece can be hung horizontally or vertically over a console table or a dresser or you can even place it over the mantel.

Boho Macramé Wall Hanging

Supplies

Jute cord or whichever kind of string for hanging your dowel to the wall

Scissors

Clothesline rope cording – you can use any cording you like. This pattern used some white clothesline rope bought from Walmart. You will need about 800 feet. This pattern used 3/16"

Wooden branch or dowel

Optional: greenery

Choices for cording

Joanne fabric

Hobby lobby

Instructions

Step one: Mount the dowel on your wall. Begin by first cutting twelve rope pieces, two body lengths. Place one tip of your rope on the left hand then stretch it towards the left. Use your right hand to hold the center of your rope then stretch towards the right. This is 1 complete body length to measure two body lengths. Clasp the tip using your right hand then once again stretch towards the left all the way using the left hand then once again extend to the left. This is now 2 body lengths. Slice the rope.

*Note: This pattern was made with 1 body length (I used 400 ft.) but would be better to use 2 so that the rope would hang longer.

Step two: Using a lark' head knot, attach the ropes to the dowel then square knot your way through.

Step three: Use the 4 middle rope strands to make a square knot. You should know and keep in mind that while you work along, you will be making a V-shape. Keep going on the right side then jump the next 2 strands of rope to make another square knot in the following four rope strands. Repeat the same procedure for the back side.

Step four: Take the 2 strands of skipped yarn and 2 rope strands from the newly made square knot. Use the 4 strands to create another square knot. Repeat the same procedure for the other side

Step five: Take 2 strands from the 2 strands of rope from the knot at the center and 2 strands from the knot at the center to make another square knot. Repeat the same process for the back side.

Step six: To mold your design into a V shape, join the sides with a square knot. Make the square knot with those 4 center strands.

Step seven: Hold the left rope strand working with the adjacent square knot which hasn't been worked yet. This is going to be the leading cord. Create a half hitch knot below one side. Use all strands down the side of the V. Repeat the same process for the remaining side.

Step nine: Using 2 strands from the preceding square knot, keep working below the side until you have three on either sides.

Step ten: Crisscross your cord of rope from the square knot and half hitch knot on either sides. This is going to bring your design together. Make one more square knot in the center to finish off.

Step eleven: To have 3 V shapes, redo this design two other times.

Step twelve: Use a spiral knot to join the V shapes. Take two rope strands from V shape the right and 2 more from the left V shape to create the spiral knot. Knot all the spirals six times. Repeat the same process for the other side.

Step thirteen: Using a lark's head knot, attach 2 other rope strands on your dowel. Create a square knot then work a spiral knot allowing a tiny ½" space from that square knot on top –five knots to be specific. Repeat the same process on the other side.

Step fourteen: Use a half hitch knot to bring everything together on all the V shapes. For this particular design, the spiral knot you just made is going to be the leading cord on the left side and you will use 2 strands from the spiral knot at the center from before. To bring it together, attach another square knot to all the points on your V.

Step fifteen: You may get as creative as you want in this step. Cut 2 rope strands and tie them to the furthest left of your dowel using a regular double knot. Drape your rope then tie it to the center of your design. Repeat the same instructions for the back side. Tie a tiny rope strand to the center lightly so that it is now draping between the 2 strands that you have just made. Attach along the strands you made using a collection of the Lark's head knot until full

Step sixteen: chop the bottom then smooth up the tips

Step seventeen: You can incorporate greenery on top or just leave it as is

DIY Macramé Chandelier

Supplies

Iron

35m of cotton rope

Scissors

Lampshade

*For this particular project we got 40 yards of 3/8 inch rope (35 meters of 0.5cm cotton 3 strands rope) which was then separated into 3 strands for a softer feel. We therefore had a total of 105m of rope (144 yards of 3/8 rope). You will need to buy 105m instead of the 35m if you do not use the 3 strand or rope or you simply don't want to unravel it.

The complete macramé project ended up with 20 cm in length for the tassel part and 25cm in length for the macramé part. (That's 8 inches for the tassel and 10 inches for the macramé). For the base, we deconstructed a cheap lampshade measuring 12 inches in diameter (30 cm). You should remove the covering so that the wire is left over. For this pattern, I left out the bottom and ended up using the light holder and the top wire frame.

Instructions

Step 1: Cut your rope first to size, 3 meters or 118 inches per piece then unravel it into 3 strands. Since you will be folding the pieces in half before you knot them to the lampshade base, the formula for working out the length of the rope is the length of the final wove chandelier multiplied by 6.

Step 2: Unravel the rope then iron it to make it straighter to get that gorgeous soft tassel look. Use a reverse lark's head knot to tie the separated pieces of rope after folding them in half first. Measure down 1 inch from the top row of knots then start to knot the first row of square knots

Step 3: After you complete the first row, measure down another 1 inch again then start knotting the 2nd row of square knots this time using alternating strands from the previous row.

To create a thick woven border at the bottom, make the next row to be 2 rows of half knots with no space in between

Step 4: Next twist half knots. Once you keep knotting, the knots will start twisting on their own; there is no trick to doing this. This pattern did 15 half knots for each and we ended up with 4 inches of long twisted pieces.

Measure and adjust the twisted pieces until all lengths are even then do 2 more rows of half knots to make the border at the bottom thicker.

Step 5: The last step is measuring the ideal length for the tassels then snipping off the excess rope.

Macrame Inspired Clay Pots

Supplies

Hot glue gun and glue sticks

Yarn in your preferred color of choice (this pattern used fun ombre yarn from Joann)

Scissors

White spray paint (with primer included)

Cardboard

Terra Cotta clay pot

Instructions

Step 1: Clean the clay pot thoroughly then allow it to dry fully. Since the clay is usually really porous, allow several hours for it to dry fully; it would be perfect if you can leave it out under the sun to dry.

Step 2: Use spray paint that is white in color to apply two coats to the pot then leave to dry

Step 3: After measuring the circumference of the pot, cut out a cardboard piece that doubles that length. Wrap the yarn around the strip of cardboard for the cardboard's whole width. Slice on one end.

Take another yarn strand and wrap it around the side to side distance of the rim of your clay pot then cut 2 inches longer than that; this will be the band which you are going to incorporate the yarn to. Loop the strand of yarn through itself to integrate the yarn to the band. Pull together tightly then cut the base to your preferred shape. Apply a thin layer of hot glue through the whole back of the band along your macramé knots.

Step 4: incorporate the band above the rim of your clay pot then tie the remaining yarn behind in a knot. Cut off the extra yarn.

*It is recommended that you slice the yarn for the pot as soon as it is secured so that you may have a clear picture of the way it is going to hang. This pattern cut out a V-shape that is wide but you may make it into a W-shape, rounded, keep it straight or whichever style you prefer

Conclusion

Macramé is a very useful craft that works well as a hobby (stress reliever) and can be a source of income. Like any other skill, it takes time to perfect but once you get the hang of it you will be making all sorts of decorations in your house and garden. As you advance on the art, you will be able to come up with your own patterns and how cool is that!

Manufactured by Amazon.ca
Bolton, ON